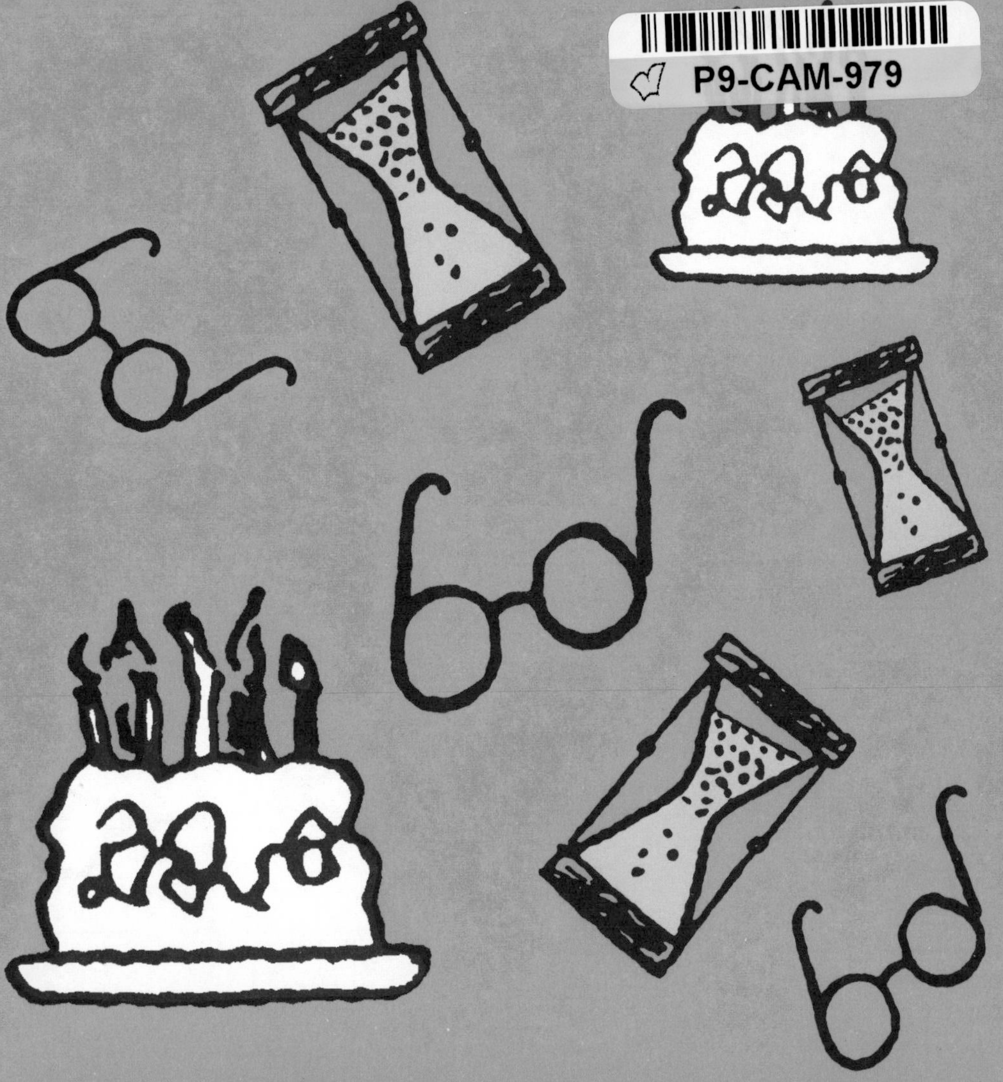

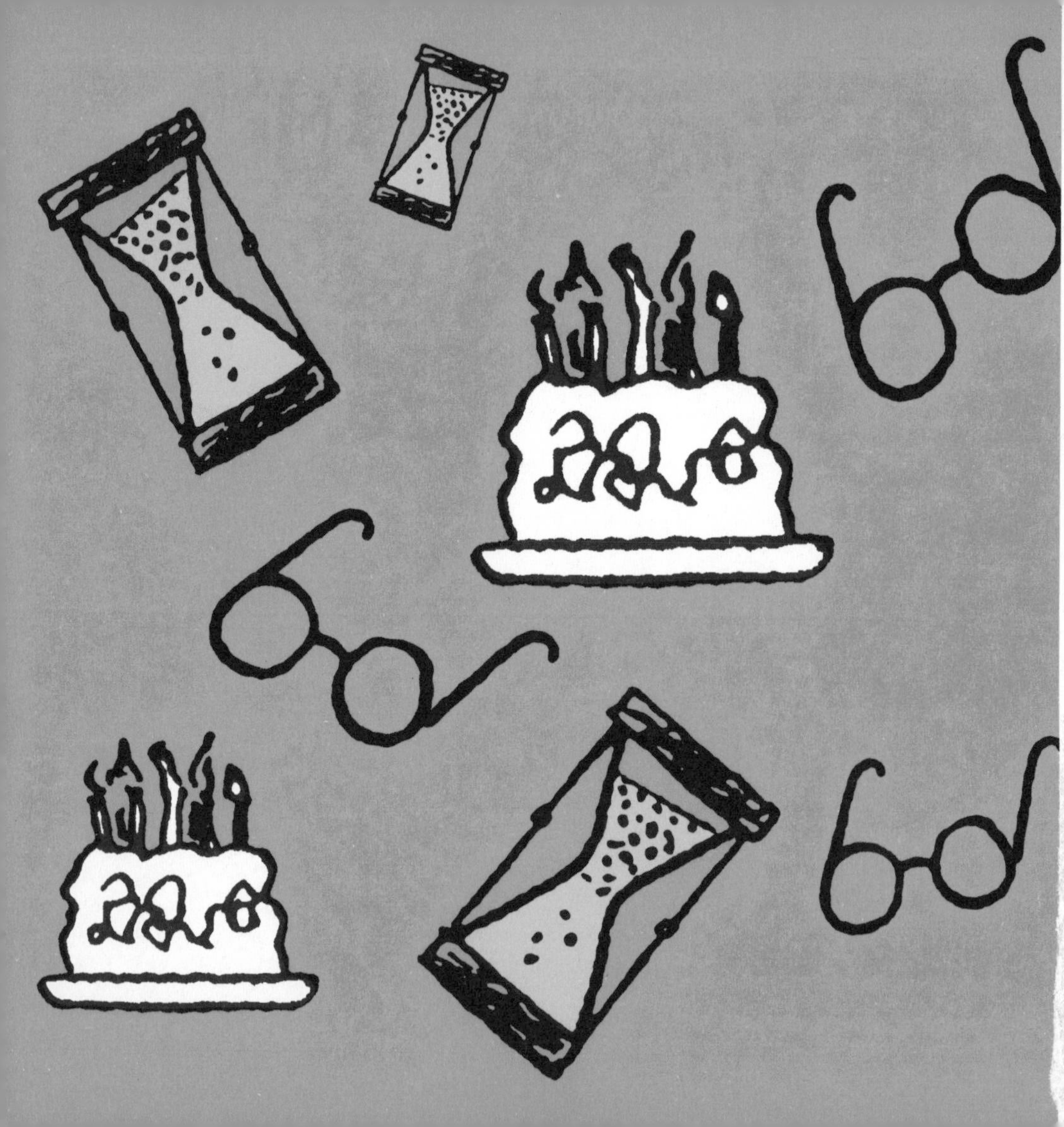

# Once You're Over The Hill

## The Hill

### (You Begin To Pick Up Speed)

*by*

*SCHULZ*

**HarperCollins***Publishers*

# Stop The Clock!

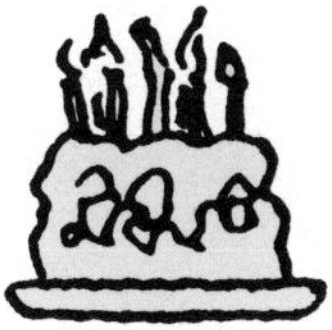

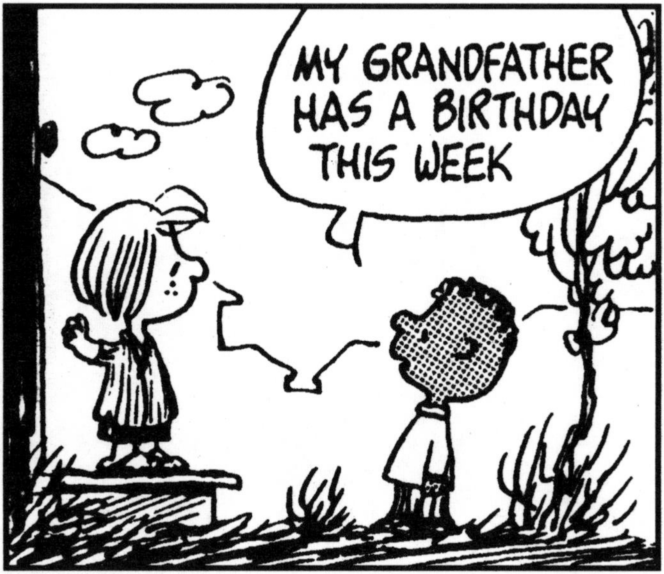
MY GRANDFATHER HAS A BIRTHDAY THIS WEEK

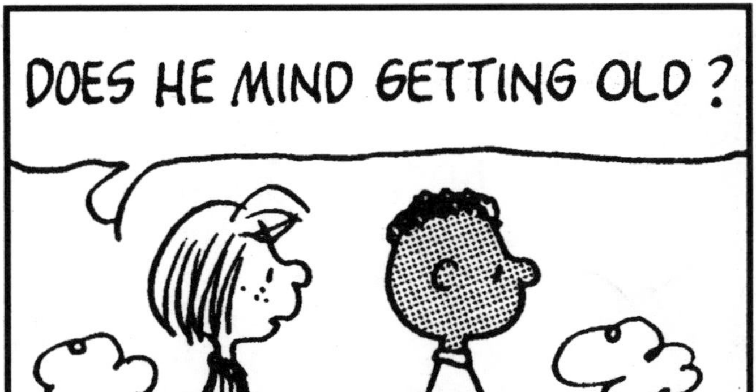
DOES HE MIND GETTING OLD?

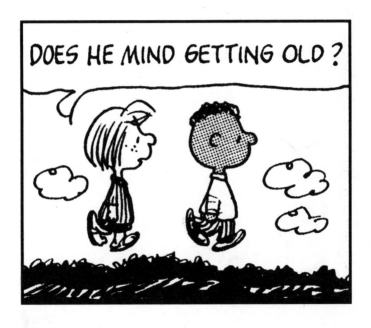

NO, HE SAYS IT DOESN'T BOTHER HIM ... IN FACT, HE SAYS HE FEELS GREAT...

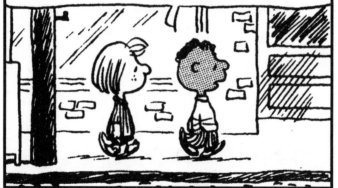

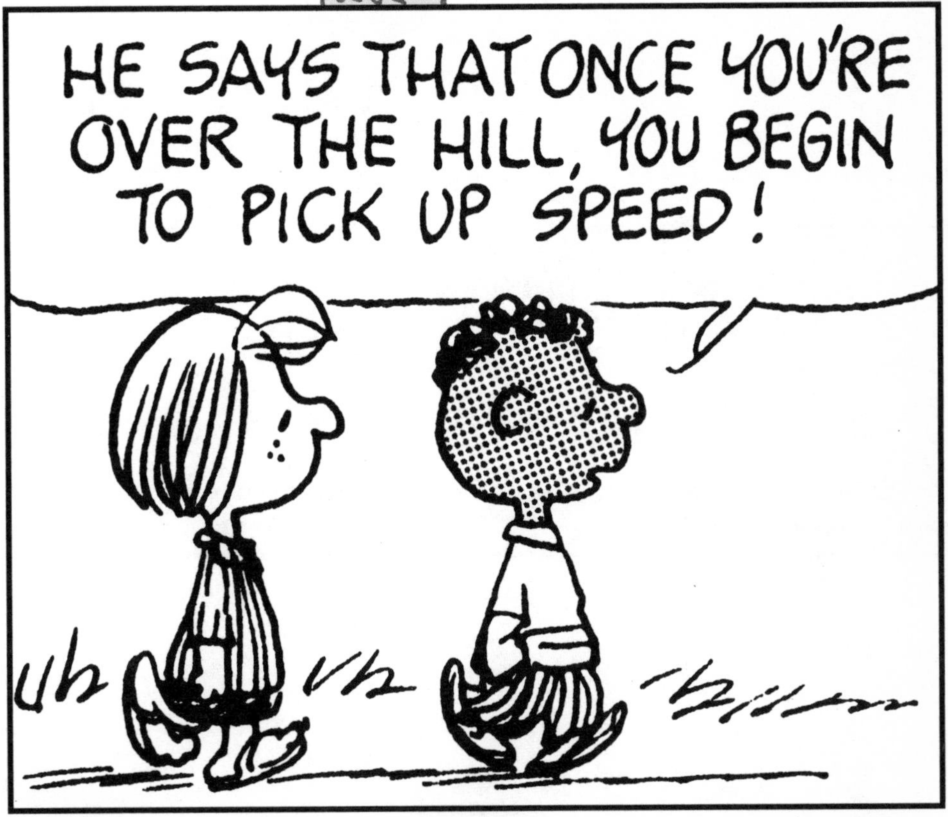
HE SAYS THAT ONCE YOU'RE OVER THE HILL, YOU BEGIN TO PICK UP SPEED!

LIFE IS GOING BY TOO FAST FOR ME
I'M NOT ACCOMPLISHING ANYTHING... I'M NOT GETTING ANYWHERE...
I'M NOT EVEN LEARNING ANYTHING...

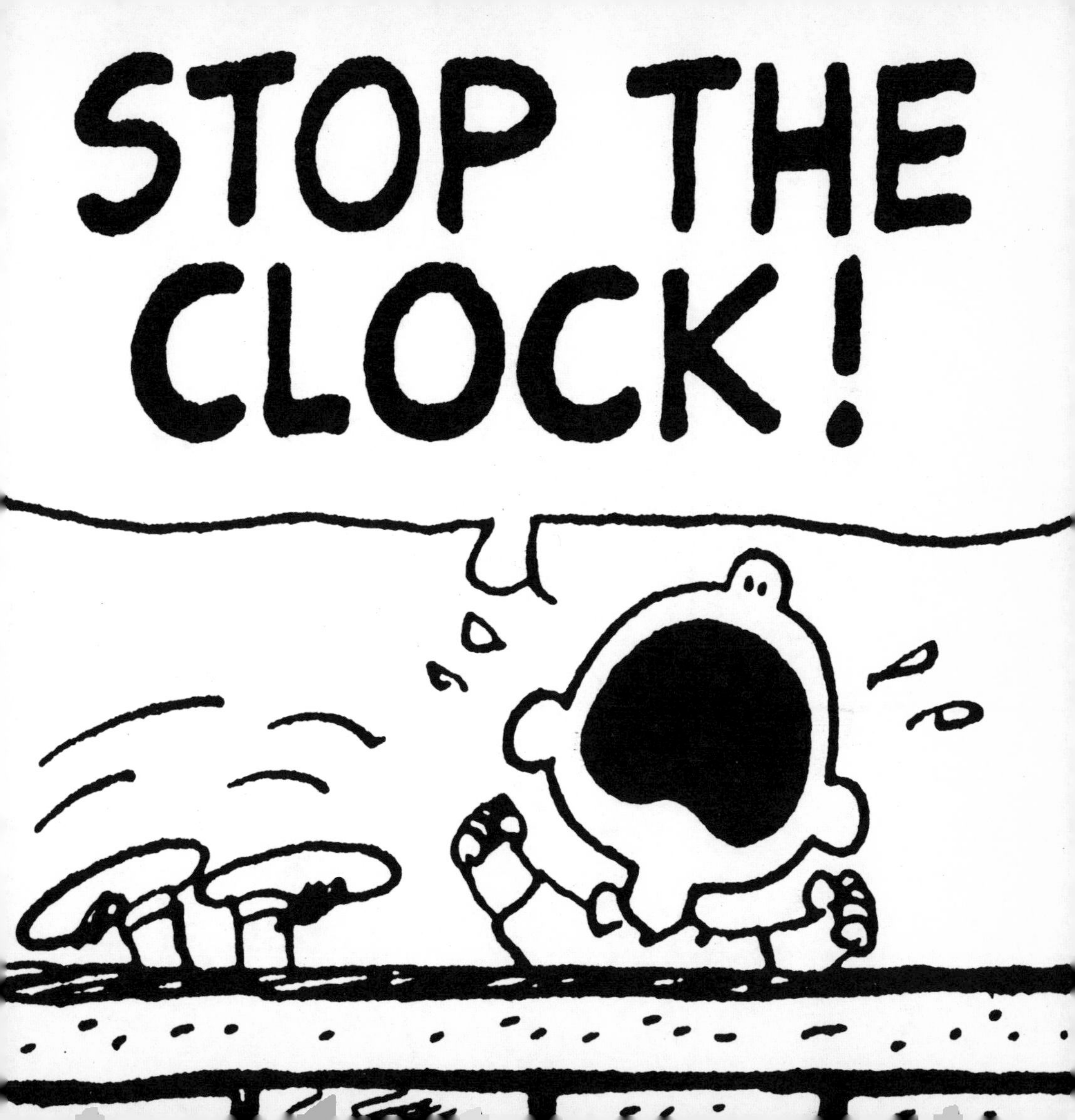
STOP THE CLOCK!

YEARS ARE LIKE SWIMMING POOLS, CHUCK...
WE JUMP IN ONE END, AND WE SPLASH AROUND UNTIL WE REACH THE OTHER END
HOW WAS YOUR YEAR, CHUCK?

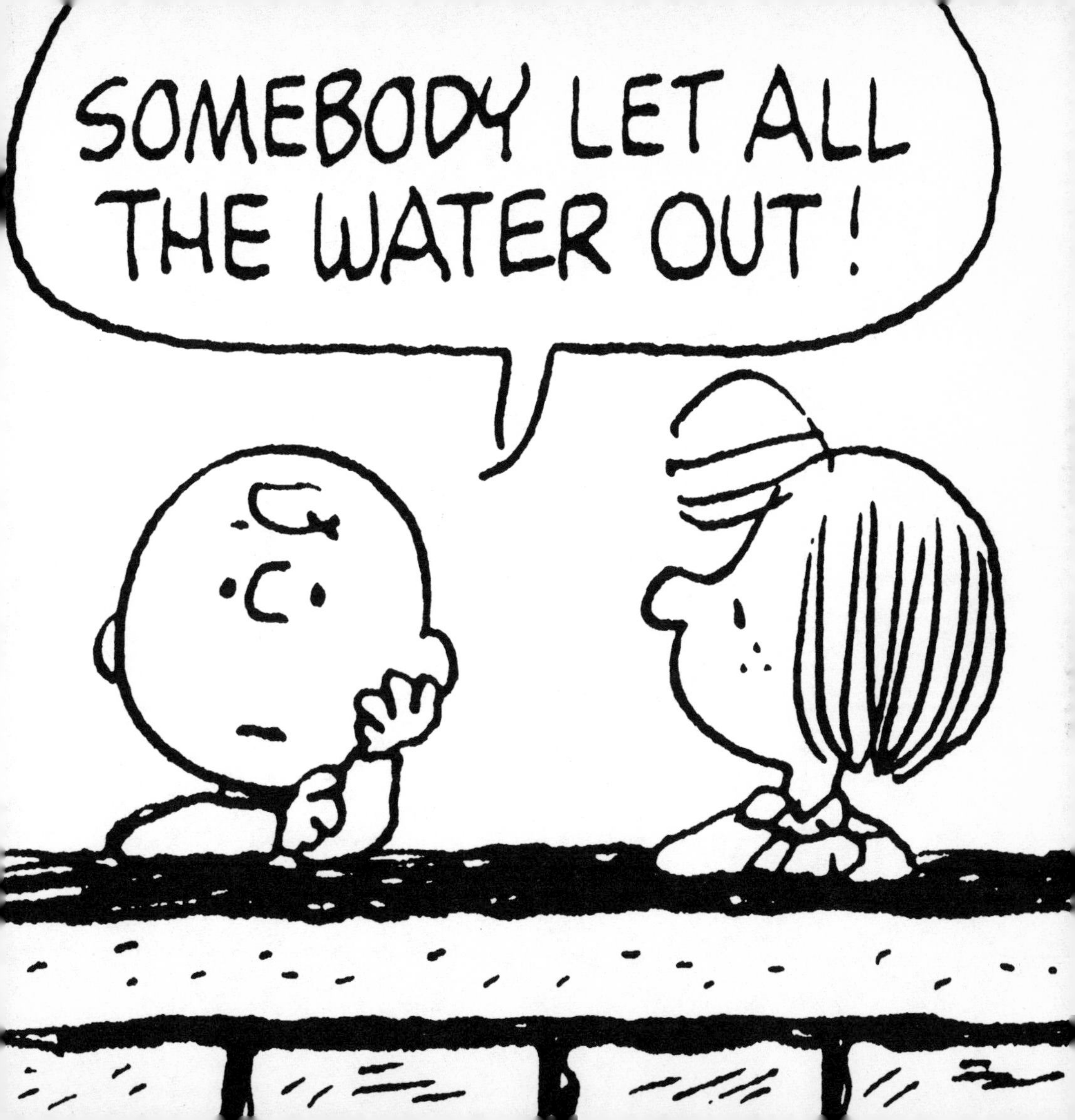
SOMEBODY LET ALL THE WATER OUT!

# Forget-Me-Nots

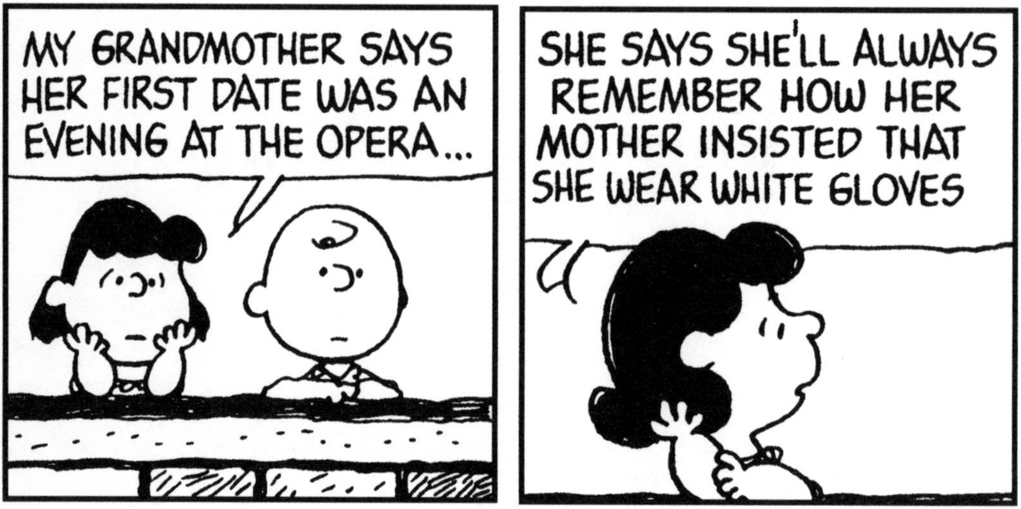
MY GRANDMOTHER SAYS HER FIRST DATE WAS AN EVENING AT THE OPERA...
SHE SAYS SHE'LL ALWAYS REMEMBER HOW HER MOTHER INSISTED THAT SHE WEAR WHITE GLOVES

HOW ABOUT HER DATE? WHO WAS THE BOY?
WHO KNOWS? ALL SHE REMEMBERS IS THE WHITE GLOVES!

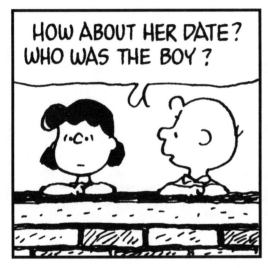

MY GRANDFATHER LOVES TO SING HYMNS
HE CAN REMEMBER THE WORDS TO OVER A HUNDRED HYMNS!
DOES HE SING IN THE CHOIR?

NO, HE CAN'T REMEMBER WHERE THE CHURCH IS..

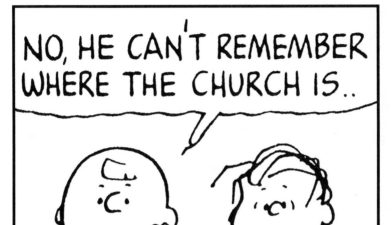

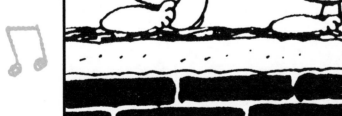

I HEAR YOUR GRAMPA JUST RETIRED...
WHAT DOES HE DO ALL DAY?
OH, HE KEEPS BUSY...

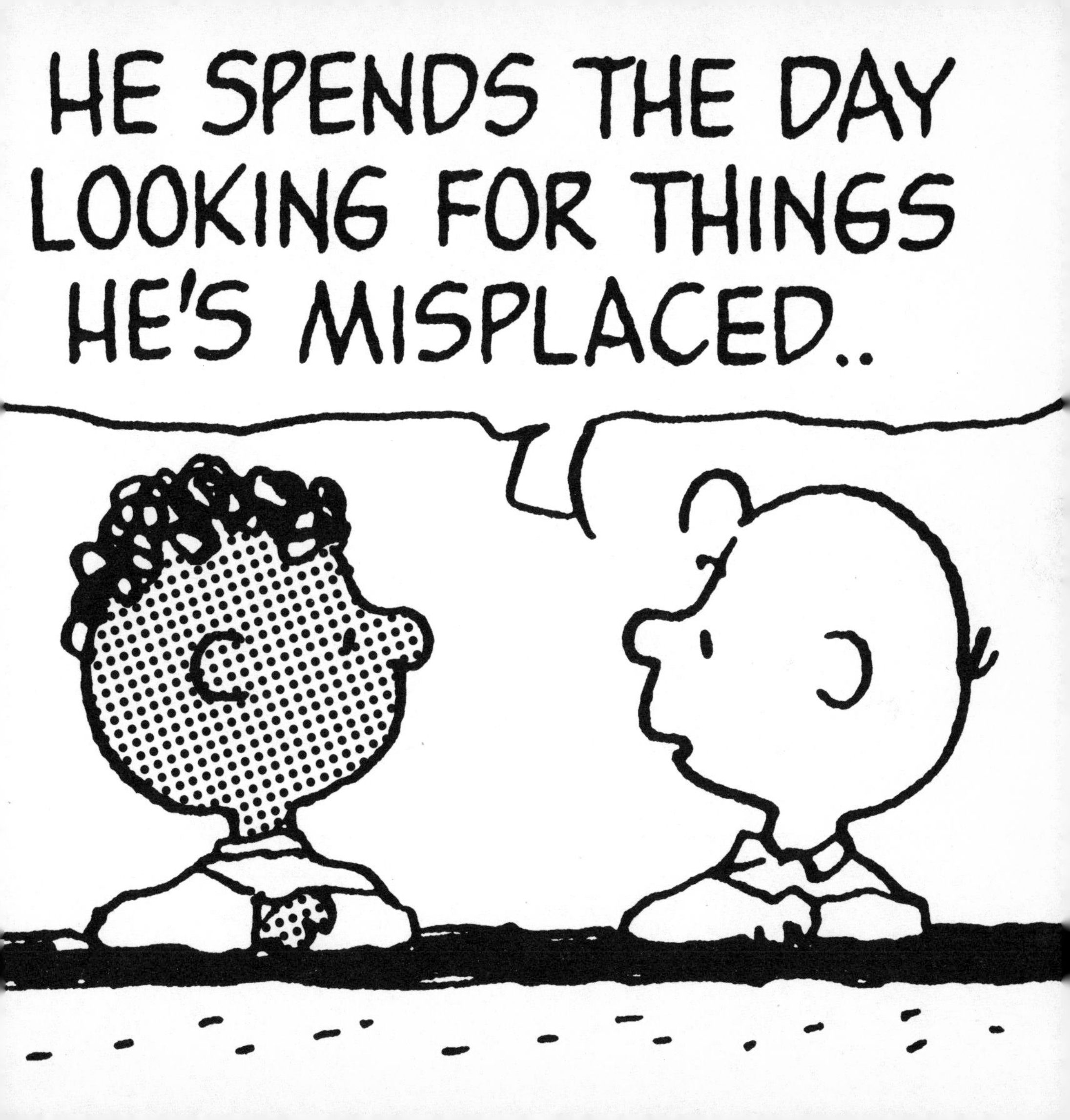
HE SPENDS THE DAY LOOKING FOR THINGS HE'S MISPLACED..

# Going Into Overtime

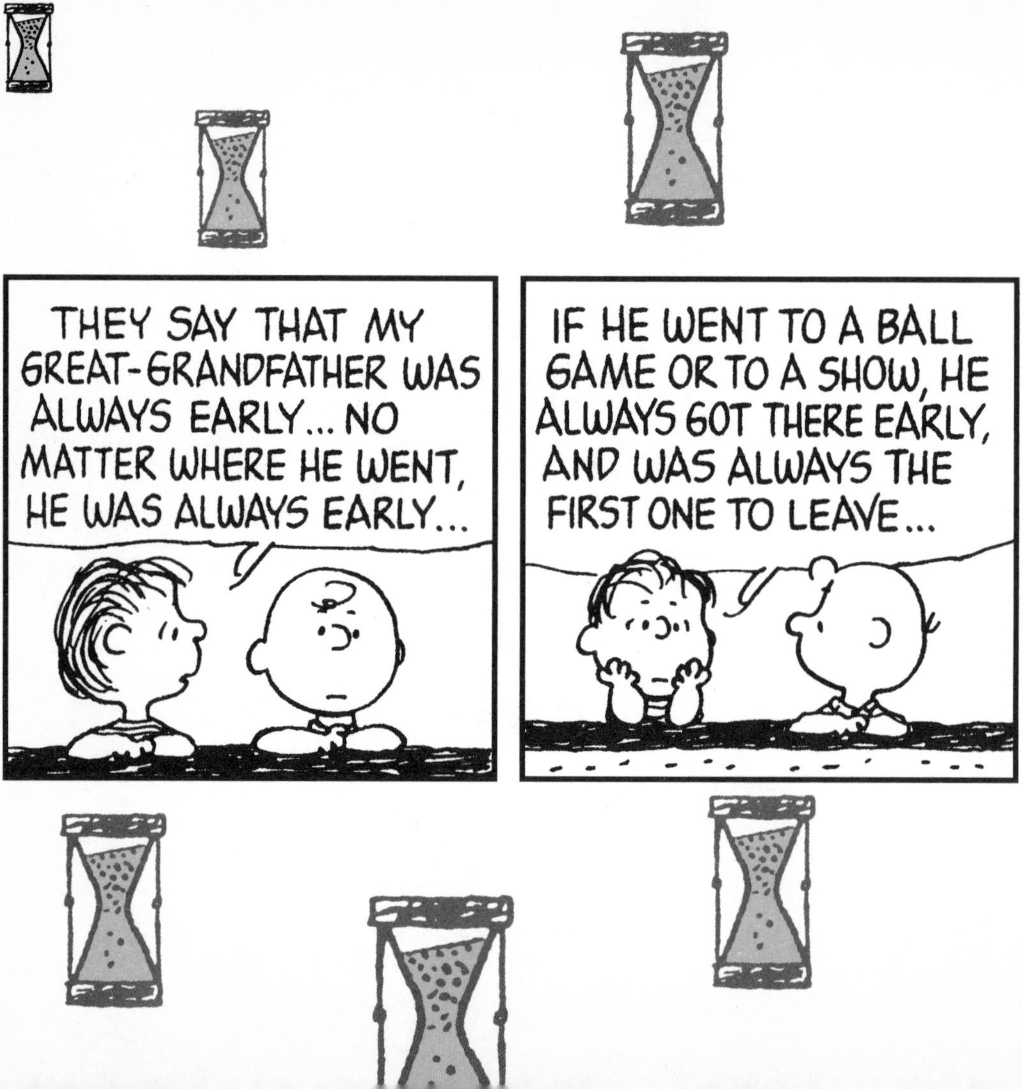
THEY SAY THAT MY GREAT-GRANDFATHER WAS ALWAYS EARLY... NO MATTER WHERE HE WENT, HE WAS ALWAYS EARLY...
IF HE WENT TO A BALL GAME OR TO A SHOW, HE ALWAYS GOT THERE EARLY, AND WAS ALWAYS THE FIRST ONE TO LEAVE...

DID HE LIVE TO A RIPE OLD AGE?
NO, HE LEFT EARLY!

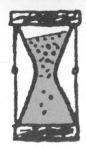

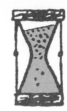

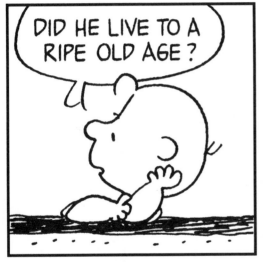

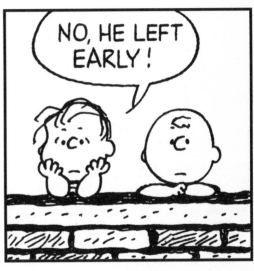

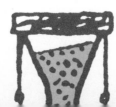

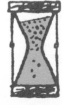

IS IT JULY ALREADY?
I CAN'T BELIEVE IT!
MY LIFE IS GOING BY TOO FAST

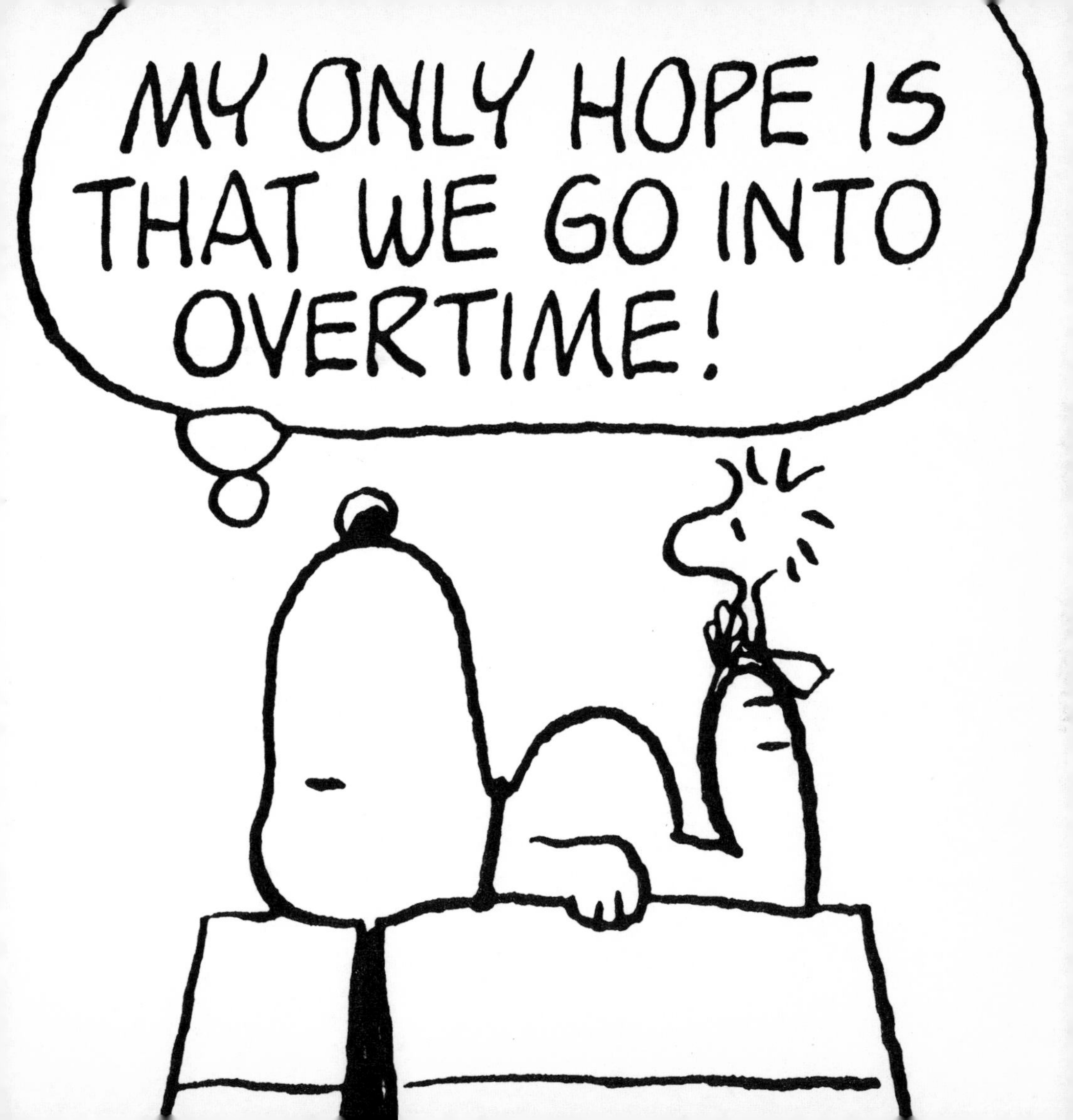
MY ONLY HOPE IS THAT WE GO INTO OVERTIME!

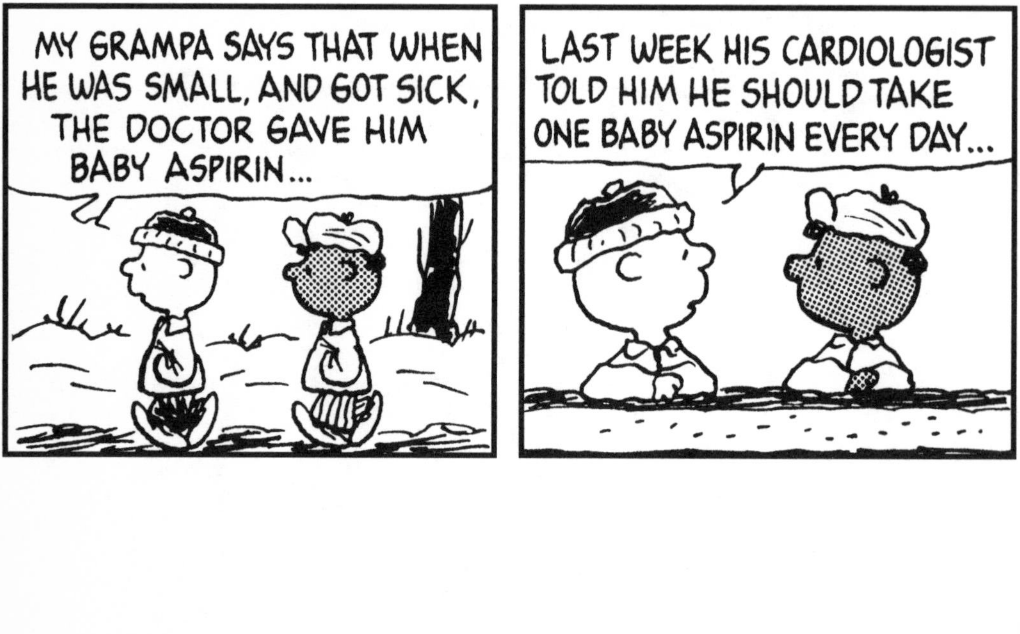
MY GRAMPA SAYS THAT WHEN HE WAS SMALL, AND GOT SICK, THE DOCTOR GAVE HIM BABY ASPIRIN...
LAST WEEK HIS CARDIOLOGIST TOLD HIM HE SHOULD TAKE ONE BABY ASPIRIN EVERY DAY...

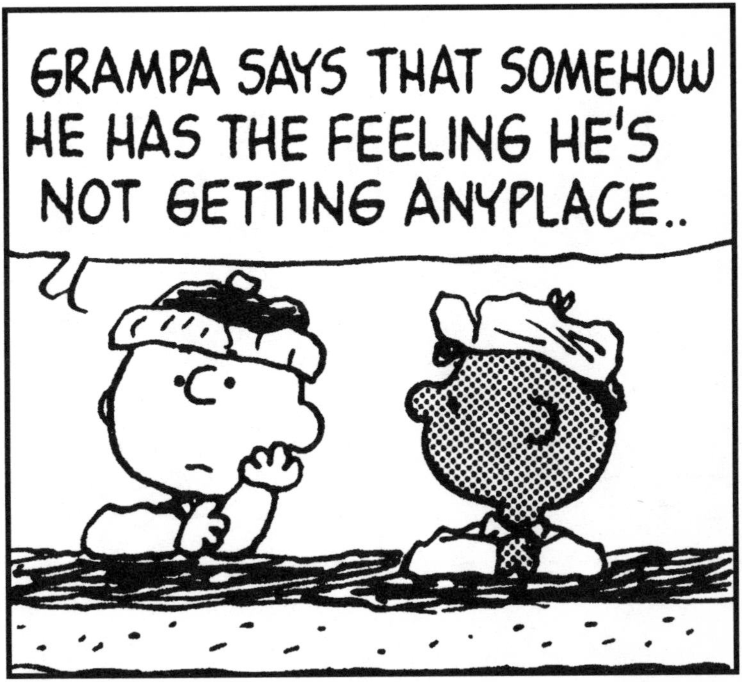
GRAMPA SAYS THAT SOMEHOW HE HAS THE FEELING HE'S NOT GETTING ANYPLACE..

GRAMMA SAYS SHE'S FOUND A NEW LITTLE RESTAURANT THAT SHE REALLY LIKES..
THEY SERVE SMALL PORTIONS..

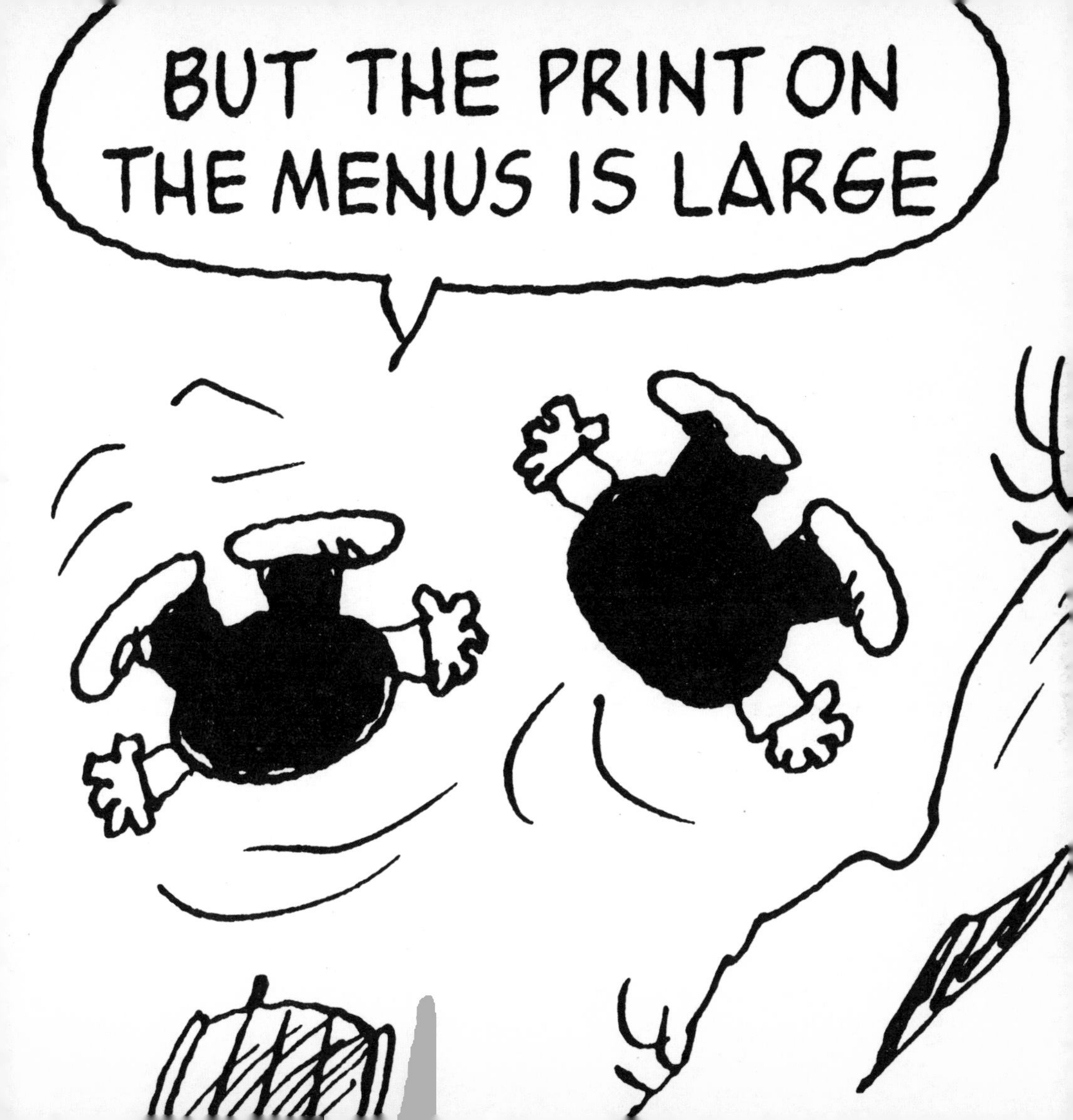
BUT THE PRINT ON THE MENUS IS LARGE

OUR NEIGHBORS HAD A NEW BABY SEVERAL MONTHS AGO.. SHE SEEMS TO BE GROWING UP SO FAST...
YESTERDAY SHE WAS CRAWLING..TOMORROW SHE'LL PROBABLY BE WALKING AND TALKING...
MY GRANDFATHER SAYS THAT'S WHAT'S GOOD ABOUT OLD PEOPLE...

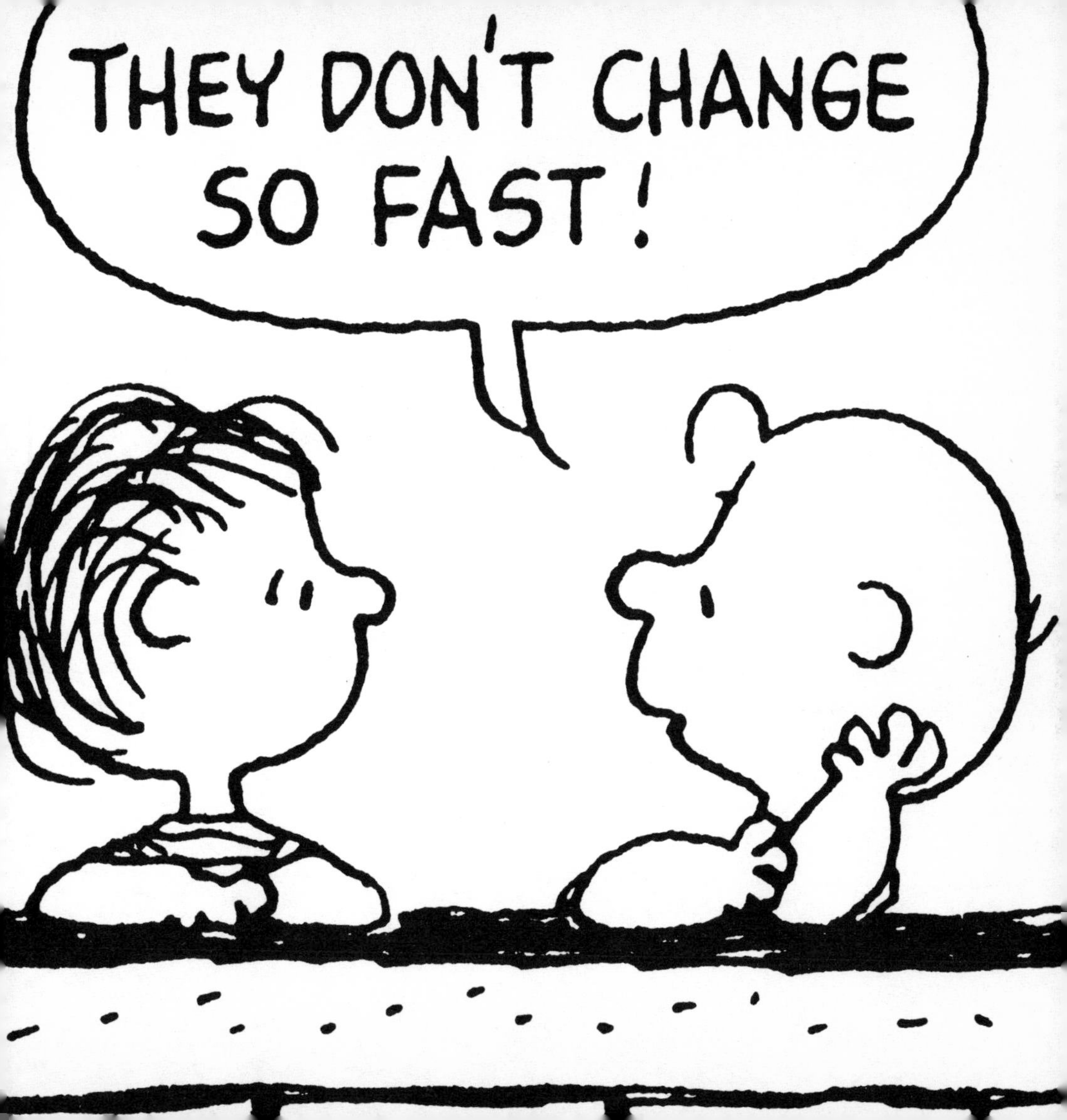
THEY DON'T CHANGE SO FAST!

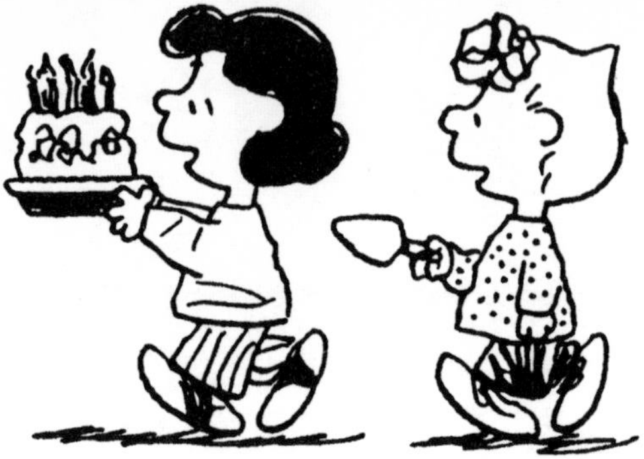

HarperCollins*Publishers*

Produced by Jennifer Barry Design, Sausalito, CA
Creative consultation by 360°, NYC.
First published in 1997 by HarperCollins*Publishers* Inc.
http://www.harpercollins.com

Based on the PEANUTS ® comic strip by Charles M. Schulz
http://www.unitedmedia.com

ISBN 0-06-757450-5

Printed in Hong Kong

1 3 5 7 9 10 8 6 4 2

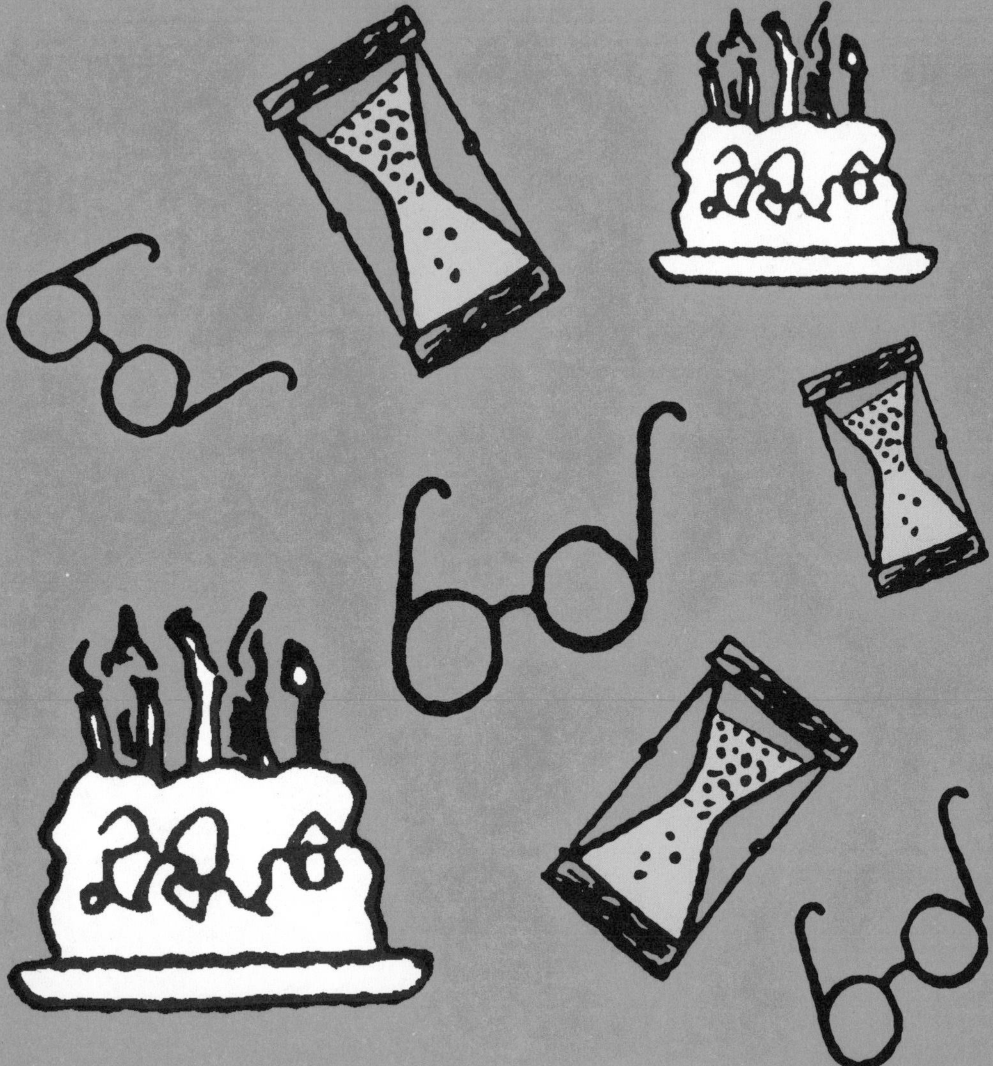

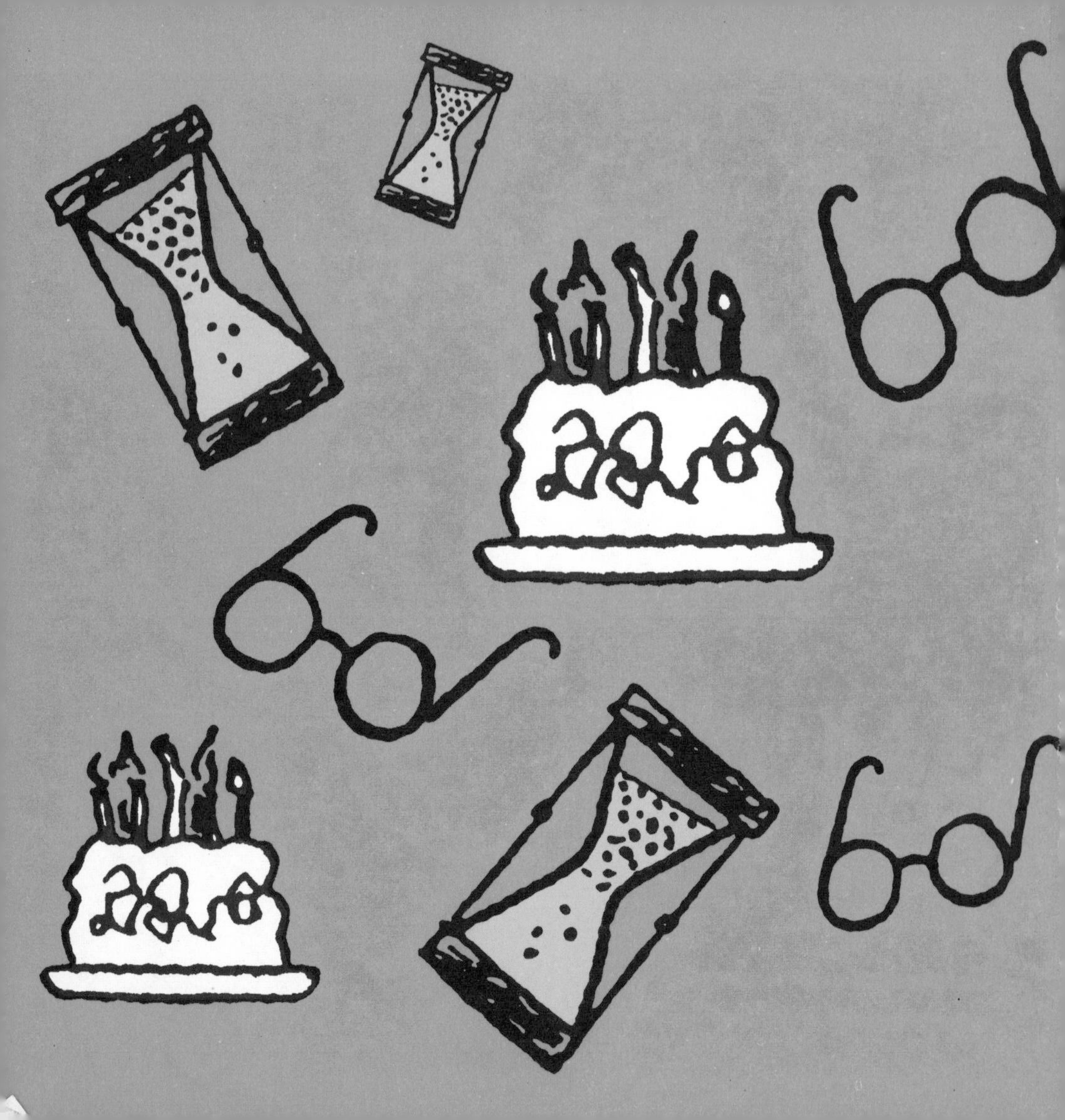